LIGHTS,

CAMERA,

ALCATRAZ

LIGHTS, CAMERA, ALCATRAZ

Hollywood's View of an American Landmark

by Dashka Slater

GOLDEN GATE NATIONAL PARKS CONSERVANCY
SAN FRANCISCO, CALIFORNIA

Library of Congress Control Number:
2003111717
ISBN 1-883869-84-6

The Golden Gate National Parks
Conservancy is a nonprofit membership
organization created to help preserve the
Golden Gate National Parks, enhance the
experiences of park visitors, and build
a community dedicated to conserving
the parks for the future. For more information, please call (415) 4R-PARKS, or
visit *www.parksconservancy.org*. Your pur-
chase of this publication helps support
the parks.

Editor: Susan Tasaki
Photo Captions: John Martini
Design: David Bullen Design

Printed on recycled paper in Hong Kong
through Global Interprint, Santa Rosa, CA

Cover: Still from *The Birdman of Alcatraz*
(United Artists, 1962; photo courtesy
Everett Collection)
Title Page: Still from *The Rock* (Hollywood
Pictures/Disney, 1996; photo courtesy
Everett Collection)

Movie posters and other ephemera, popular
with collectors, are in wide circulation; a
few posters are included here to illustrate
the various ways Hollywood used Alcatraz as
a symbol and evoked its atmosphere. Through
the years, posters for movies with an Alcatraz
connection had a number of points in common:
Guns or other weapons are prominent in most
of them, as are cell bars and worried expres-
sions. Strong-jawed determination is also popular (*Road to Alcatraz,* p. 5, and *The Rock,* p. 57).
In the poster for *Birdman of Alcatraz* (p. 51),
Lancaster's haunted expression, the bars, and
the birds flying free imply a man's struggle
against those who would imprison his soul;
in *Murder in the First* (p. 67), Alcatraz's dehuman-
izing effect is reflected in the position adopted
by Henry Young (Kevin Bacon). With few excep-
tions (one of which is *House Across the Bay,* p. 41),
the mood is violent, confrontational, or both. Of
the posters reproduced in this book, only one
shows a lively sense of the absurd (*Skidoo,* p. 72).

Alcatraz: A Place, an Image, a Myth

INTRODUCTION BY RICH WEIDEMAN

Chief, Public Affairs
Golden Gate National Recreation Area
National Park Service

RIKER'S ISLAND. ROBBEN ISLAND. TERMINAL ISLAND. McNEIL ISLAND. DEVIL'S ISLAND. ALCATRAZ ISLAND.

John Donne wrote, "No man is an island." Yet plenty of men—and women—have been imprisoned on one. In the world-wide history of crime and punishment, islands figure large in society's choices for places of incarceration, especially for high-profile or high-security prisoners.

Why? They provide a physical distance from the "law-abiding" members of society. They're relatively easy to secure. There's a real sense of psychological separation from the mainstream. Their resources, or lack of them, make them impractical for other uses. Speculatively speaking, all of these could be reasons for using islands as prison sites.

In the United States, the name of one particular island has come to symbolize all that is harsh and grim: Alcatraz. The name conjures up an image of the worst prison in America, if not the world. Today, more than three decades after it closed as a penal institution, Alcatraz draws in excess of 1.4 million visitors annually. They come from all corners of the globe to see the cells of Al Capone, the Birdman, and Machine Gun Kelly, to name just a few.

Back in 1972, the island was designated a National Historic Landmark and incorporated into the newly created Golden Gate National Recreation Area. Within a year, the National Park Service had done what it could to make

it ready for public visitation, including training NPS interpreters and preparing them to lead tours in this most unusual national park site. They didn't think the duty posting would last long, however. NPS planners estimated that it would take perhaps five years for the pub-

The public's fascination with USP Alcatraz shows no sign of waning; each year, more than 1.4 million people visit the island, tour the cellhouse, and discover the difference between myth and history. *(Photo by and courtesy Brenda Tharp)*

lic's interest in the prison to be satisfied. By the late 1970s, they thought, everyone interested in the island would've seen it and they might have to close it due to lack of interest. Was the NPS in for a rude awaking? Yes!

As Dashka Slater demonstrates in this book, a large part of what keeps Alcatraz in the psyche of the public is the entertainment industry, especially Hollywood, which has woven it into the fabric of American history through the medium of film. In every decade since Alcatraz opened as a federal prison in 1934, movies—and later, television—have taken advantage of our interest in what we perceive to be the unknown world of a desolate island lockup.

The drawing power of Alcatraz started early. As US Penitentiary Alcatraz, it was off-limits to the public, and unless you lived, worked, or had official business there, you were forbidden to visit. This prohibition naturally generated intense curiosity as to what was happening on the island. Alcatraz viewing scopes were set up on Fisherman's Wharf, and tour boats circled the island . . . but not too closely! Reporters waited at the dock for newly released prisoners, whom they would interview so they could provide their readers with all the colorful details of prison life. Needless to say, many of the details were far more colorful in the telling than they were in actuality. Now that Alcatraz is a National Park Service site, the public is welcomed, and the island's power to attract the curious continues unabated.

The modern-day surge in

interest started in 1979 with the filming and international release of *Escape from Alcatraz*, starring Clint Eastwood. This successful film, and others that have followed, seem to guarantee the island's ongoing appeal. When overseas tour operators suggest visits to the US, especially to the West Coast, a handful of destinations are considered "must-see" sites: Yosemite, Grand Canyon, Disneyland, the Golden Gate Bridge, and Alcatraz are at the top of the icon list. All carry huge name recognition in the international community.

When I started as a National Park Service guide on Alcatraz in the summer of 1981, I was struck by this level of international

Burt Lancaster as Robert Stroud in the *Birdman of Alcatraz*. This highly acclaimed production included a tour-de-force portrayal by Lancaster and spurred a public outcry for Stroud's release, but ignored virtually all of the real Stroud's homicidal and pathological behaviors; see p. 46 for a photo of Stroud, who bears no resemblence to Lancaster or to the gentle nature implied in this photograph. *(United Artists, 1962; photo courtesy Everett Collection)*

interest in Alcatraz. Not a day went by that I didn't hear at least twenty different languages spoken on the Rock. No matter what the language, however, the questions tended to be similar: *Where is Clint Eastwood's cell? Where did the Birdman keep his birds? Did anyone escape from the island?* Now, after giving tours of Alcatraz for more than twenty years, I continue to hear the same questions, asked not only by twelve-year-olds from the American Midwest, but also by heads of state, presidents, first ladies, and movie stars, to name a few.

Interest in Alcatraz cuts across economic, social, and geographic borders. On a typical summer day, more than 5,000 disappointed people may be turned away. The carrying capacity of the ferries, as well as the island staff's capacity to effectively interact with visitors, restricts daily visitation to approximately 4,000 people. When that number of tickets have been sold, sales end for the day.

When you visit the island, be prepared to discover the real Alcatraz, the verifiable history of this former prison island. Audio tours, NPS rangers, and interpreters debunk the myths and provide information that will help you draw your own conclusions about the nature of Alcatraz. The most important chapter in the history of Alcatraz is still being written as the island is preserved, protected, and restored for future generations; as its visitors gain insight into life behind bars; and as the differences between real life and reel life are made clear.

Much like today, San Franciscans in the 1960s complained about the "carnival appearance and ballyhoo" at Fisherman's Wharf. Here, tourists peer through coin-operated telescopes aimed at Alcatraz and hope for a glimpse of the penitentiary and its residents. *(Photo courtesy San Francisco History Center, San Francisco Public Library, AAC-9285)*

LIGHTS, CAMERA, ALCATRAZ

In 1981, seventeen years after the federal government shut down its penitentiary on Alcatraz Island, a new Alcatraz prison opened for business. Like the old Alcatraz, this new Alcatraz featured two tiers of cramped 5-by-9-foot cells, along with a mess hall and a segregation unit for those prisoners who disobeyed the rules. Every detail of the new prison replicated the old, even the shape of the rivets and texture of the cell walls. But there were some important differences. Instead of being forged from tool-proof case-hardened

steel, the bars on the new cells were made of flimsy metal tubing. And instead of sitting on twenty-two acres of sandstone in the middle of San Francisco Bay, the new Alcatraz took up ten thousand feet of warehouse space in Culver City, California.

Culver City's Alcatraz is a movie set, originally constructed for the Clint Eastwood film *Escape from Alcatraz*, modified and enlarged for a Paul Krasny-directed television two-parter called *Alcatraz: The Whole Shocking Story*, and then purchased by GMT Studios and made into a permanent sound stage. The mess hall and segregation unit no longer exist, but the replica of cell block C has

been in use for more than twenty years, providing Alcatraz ambience for hundreds of movies, television shows, commercials, and music videos.

It is rare for a Hollywood set to last even a few weeks after a film is complete; for one to last decades is practically unheard-of. But Hollywood has always had an unusual love affair with the Rock. In the seventy years

Convicts, anonymous in the shadows, kill time in their second tier cells along Broadway. Most Alcatraz inmates had jobs, but men not assigned to work details spent up to 23 hours a day in their cells, the tedium broken only by three 20-minute meals. *(Photo courtesy San Francisco History Center, San Francisco Public Library, AAC-9372)*

DEATH...if the drug proves fatal!
FREEDOM ...if their gamble wins!

CAN THIS DRUG DRIVE MEN TO MURDER?

RKO presents

Experiment Alcatraz

starring
JOHN HOWARD · JOAN DIXON

Produced and Directed by EDWARD L. CAHN
Screenplay by ORVILLE H. HAMPTON
From a Screenplay by
GEORGE W. GEORGE and GEORGE F. SLAVIN

Copyright 1950 RKO Radio Pictures Inc. Country of Origin U.S.A.

since it first opened as a federal penitentiary, Alcatraz has been the subject of more than two dozen movies, and it has made guest appearances in many more. There have been prison movies, horror movies, comedies, romances, action films, kids' movies, even "adult" flicks set on Alcatraz. The island's distinctive wind-swept silhouette is the obvious draw, but its eerie soundtrack has had a successful movie career as well. The sound of the cell doors closing is catalogued in the Lucas Films sound library, providing a menacing and irrevocable slam in such movies as *The Empire Strikes Back, Jurassic Park,* and *Terminator 2.*

THE ROCK. Hellcatraz. America's Devil's Island. In the symbolic language of cinema, Alcatraz is hell on earth: hopeless, cold, and desolate, a place where dreams go to die. In movie after movie, Hollywood has summed up the Alcatraz legend in a somber voiceover or a few pithy sentences superimposed over a shot of the wave-lashed island. "ALCATRAZ. America's penal fortress, grim and mysterious as its name—where cold steel and rushing tides protect civilization from its enemies." (*Alcatraz Island,* 1937) "The Rock. A little iron curtain world of lost souls sitting in the shadow of the Golden Gate." (*Experiment Alcatraz,* 1950) "Alcatraz. An escape-proof prison for confining the deadliest murderers in the country's history." (*The Big Train,* 1961) "Alcatraz, a maximum security prison containing the most dangerous criminals in America." (*Birdman of Alcatraz,* 1962) "Alcatraz was the most feared prison in the world." (*Murder in the First,* 1995)

This is the Alcatraz that the vast majority of the island's 1.4 million annual visitors expect to encounter—a dark and forbidding dungeon haunted by disturbed and desperate men. They want to see where the Birdman of Alcatraz kept his birds, visit the underground tunnels featured in *The Rock,* or the brutal dungeon from *Murder in the First.* For years, Alcatraz rangers fielded inquiries about "Ranger Vickie," the prison guard-turned-tour guide played by Phil Hartman in *So I Married an Ax Murderer* (1993). Vickie, like the tunnels and the birds, is the invention of a Hollywood scriptwriter and, like many of Hollywood's Alcatraz myths, has taken on a life of his own. The Alcatraz of cinema is not the same as the real Alcatraz, nor is it meant to be. But Hollywood's Alcatraz does tell us a lot about the myth of Alcatraz, a myth that is as old as the prison itself.

THE VEIL OF SECRECY
Cultivating the Alcatraz Mystique

From the day it opened in August 1934, the federal penitentiary at Alcatraz Island had a dramatic, even glamorous image, one that the Federal Bureau of Prisons (BOP) took pains to cultivate. This was to be a prison like no other, a high-tech, escape-proof, super-maximum prison for the nation's worst criminals, and it was in the most visible place imaginable: smack in the middle of scenic San Francisco Bay. "Its buildings and towers . . . at times appear like an ancient forbidding fortress; at times like a gigantic battleship moored in the swirling cross-current a mile-and-a-half from the mainland," as described in an uncharacteristically lyrical BOP 1960 annual report. "From the city's hills and bridges; from ships passing through the Golden Gate; from every point of vantage, travelers from far and near gaze at the fabled isle and wonder. . . "

The gawkers had plenty to wonder about. From its inception, Alcatraz was shrouded in

what newspaper reporters referred to as "a veil of secrecy." Journalists toured the facility just before the first inmates arrived in August 1934, but after that the island was strictly off-limits to the public—except when a dramatic escape attempt or a prison riot forced prison officials to answer reporters' questions.

The rationale behind the secrecy was that the nation's famed gangsters needed to be taken down a peg. J. Edgar

August 18, 1934. Warden James A. Johnston shows off the newly refurbished Alcatraz cellblocks shortly after the first prisoners arrived at the penitentiary. From left to right, San Francisco Mayor Angelo Rossi, US Attorney General Homer Cummings, Warden Johnston, and San Francisco Police Chief William Quinn. *(Photo courtesy Golden Gate National Recreation Area, Park Archives, Don Denevi Collection, P83-144.060n)*

With Alcatraz as a backdrop, a cable car climbs an amazingly car-free stretch of Hyde Street hill. The large sign visible on Angel Island just above the prison reads "Welcome Home. Well Done," a greeting to returning GIs that dates this photo to late 1945 or early 1946. *(Photo courtesy San Francisco History Center, San Francisco Public Library, AAB-4062)*

Hoover's G-men were winning the war on crime, breaking up rackets and gunning down thugs, but they were losing the publicity war. Even in prison, Al Capone was a celebrity who lolled about in silk underwear and issued orders to underlings on the outside. The solution, the feds reasoned, was total isolation and total anonymity. At Alcatraz, Capone and his ilk would become "forgotten men."

ALCATRAZ Warden James A. Johnston refused to give reporters the names of inmates or release any details about their welfare. Prison officials edited and retyped all incoming and outgoing mail, excising any references to prison life and current affairs. These topics were also off limits during conversations with the visitors who spoke to inmates by telephone from the other side of a glass barricade. Inmates could only be visited by members of their immediate family or their lawyers, and then only once a month. No one else was allowed anywhere near the island. Pleasure boats that drifted within 200 yards of shore received a stern warning through a megaphone, followed, if they didn't change course, by a shot across the bow.

The secrecy, combined with the notoriety of inmates like Capone and Machine-Gun Kelly, was enough to guarantee the island's box-office draw. Any tidbit of infor-

Warden James A. Johnston in his office in the administration wing of the prison. Johnston, a noted prison reformer, had cleaned up California state penitentiaries at San Quentin and Folsom before being named warden of the federal government's new "super Bastille" in 1933. Johnston served as Alcatraz's warden from 1933 to 1948. *(Photo courtesy San Francisco History Center, San Francisco Public Library, AAD-2860)*

The visiting room at Alcatraz was originally a sterile chamber sparsely furnished with government-issue furniture and toolproof steel bars. Attorneys and convicts used the table at center for face-to-face meetings, but family members were required to sit at the booths at left for their monthly telephone visits, separated by several inches of bulletproof glass from their husbands, sons, or fathers. *(Photo courtesy Golden Gate National Recreation Area, Park Archives, Betty Wallar Collection, P83-170.193)*

"Warning—Keep Off" signs were prominently displayed along the island's perimeter. Guards patrolling catwalks and gun towers rigorously enforced a 200-yard limit for all vessels passing the island. *(Photo by and courtesy Roy Eisenhardt)*

mation about Alcatraz was news. Tour boats circled the island from a safe distance. Vendors set up telescopes on Fisherman's Wharf and offered tourists a peek through the lens. In 1936, newspapers reported that Alcatraz guards had fired on an airplane that had been seen circling the island. The airmen, the *San Francisco Examiner* reported, were "attempting to take motion pictures of prisoners."

Reporters hung about the docks, waiting for released convicts to land. The resulting interviews were the source of a steady stream of "Inside Alcatraz" accounts. With headlines like "Bad Men Tamed," "Freed Convict Describes Violence and Madness," and

"Felons' Dread of Alcatraz Dungeon Told," the articles emphasized the prison's harshness and brutality— the excruciating rule of silence, the absence of privileges, the dank "Spanish dungeons" where prisoners were sent for disobeying rules. Reporters who had seen Alcatraz for themselves had described it as "Light, airy, cheerfully decorated, and warm," but these articles conjured a far gloomier image.

"When you break a rule, and sometimes you do it just to cut loose or go nuts, they put you in the hole. It's an underground cell, cold, dark as midnight and without a thing in it, not even a mattress," reads a typical account. "When you first go in, they give you a piece of bread

and a cup of water in the morning. You get the same rations again at night, and that's all. Sometimes they forget about you for a couple of days."

Many, if not most, of these accounts were embellished, of course, and some of the more lurid tales were pure fabrication. Alcatraz was tough but it was not barbaric. Inmates were guaranteed no privileges other than food, shelter, clothing, and med-

An aging neon sign at Fisherman's Wharf still invites visitors to view Alcatraz through a battery of coin-operated telescopes. Until the 1970s, this was the closest most tourists could come to the mysterious island. *(Photo courtesy Golden Gate National Recreation Area, Craig Glassner, photographer)*

The interior of a new solitary confinement cell in remodeled D-Block, taken shortly after completion in 1940. These cells were a vast improvement over the aging army cells that had previously been used for segregation, which included below-ground solitary cells, the officially designated "dungeons." *(Photo courtesy San Francisco History Center, San Francisco Public Library, AAC-9380)*

ical attention; everything else—work, exercise, visitors—had to be earned. Minor infractions—failing to finish the food on your plate, talking while in the cellhouse, sassing a guard—brought a swift reduction in privileges. More serious violations—taking a swing at a guard for instance—could send prisoners to the pitch-black darkness of "the hole," and particularly obstreperous prisoners might on occasion be hosed down with cold water from the bay, a practice that earned Warden Johnston the nickname "Saltwater" Johnston.

But Alcatraz also boasted better conditions than many of the prisons of its time. Inmates had their own cells, an improvement over bunking with another con. Each cell had its own light and running water, and prisoners could order as many books as they wanted from the prison library. The cellhouse was heated to 70 degrees, although the bare concrete walls and constant drafts made it feel colder. The food was tasty and you could eat as much as you wanted. Johnston expected strict adherence to his rules, but he was also known as a reformer who had banned corporal punishment while running Folsom Prison.

EVEN BEFORE the New Deal, Franklin Delano Roosevelt's 1930s-era program to reinvig-

The chow line in the mess hall during the 1940s featured a menu board listing the day's specials, flanked by a pair of blackboards used for posting the latest sports scores. The rule on portions was "Take all you want but eat all you take." *(Photo courtesy Golden Gate National Recreation Area, Park Archives, Betty Wallar Collection, P83-170.228)*

The view of Alcatraz's dock from an approaching vessel during the last days of the army's Disciplinary Barracks. The lighthouse and commandant's residence (soon to become the warden's house) crown the island, while a three-story guard barracks looms over the dock. The latter was later converted to staff housing for the penitentiary's correctional officers and their families. *(Photo courtesy San Francisco History Center, San Francisco Public Library, AAC-9362)*

orate the American economy and reorder its social and political priorities, a reformist mood had swept the penal system. Rehabilitation was the credo of the newly created Federal Bureau of Prisons, which had started introducing reforms not long after its inception in 1930. Alcatraz, oddly enough, was an outgrowth of that credo. Reform could only happen, Bureau officials argued, if first-time offenders and run-of-the-mill crooks were isolated from the corrupting influence of incorrigible troublemakers, escape artists, gang leaders, and racketeers. These men were not susceptible to reform, the thinking went, at least not until they had been whittled down to size. That was the task assigned to Alcatraz.

Alcatraz thus had two contradictory images. To Warden Johnston and his superiors at the Bureau of Prisons, the facility was a monument to modern penology. The leg irons, beatings, and indefinite stays in the hole that defined life in most state prisons were not part of the Alcatraz regime; to Johnston, they were relics of a more primitive era. His Alcatraz used modern science to control its prisoners: high-tech gadgetry like metal detectors and automatic tear gas dispensers, and up-to-date theories on inmate management and discipline. "There

A correctional officer operating the metal detector, also known as a "snitch box," at the island's registration building on the dock, 1956. Much like airport security today, visitors to Alcatraz had to pass through the metal detector before ascending to the main prison. Pockets were emptied of all metal items, which were reclaimed upon departure from the island. *(Photo courtesy San Francisco History Center, San Francisco Public Library, AAC-9447)*

are no cruelties, no tortures, no corporal punishments," Johnston told a group of lawyers in 1939. "There is no laxity, no helter-skelter running around, no soft soaping . . . there is strict adherence to the necessary routine."

Yet despite these modern trappings, most people thought of Alcatraz as something out of the Dark Ages, a back-to-basics combination of Devil's Island and the Tower of London. That, in fact, was what most people wanted Alcatraz to be.

"Let other prisons that will experiment with kind treatment and other means of rehabilitation install honor systems and test psychological theories," the *San Francisco Examiner* opined when the prison opened. "Alcatraz aims to keep prisoners securely behind bars, as remote from the possibility of escape as from contacts with the outside world." Newspapers were happy to publish reports of the strain Alcatraz prisoners were feeling under the island's tight restrictions, but these were often appended with a gesture of editorial approval. "To date there has been no actual insanity and despite several attempts there have been no suicides," concluded a 1936 story detailing an inmate's accusations that Alcatraz was driving prisoners insane. "Alcatraz hurts but it works."

All the same, the Bureau of Prisons did little to contradict the prison's reputation as a house of horrors. After all, the rumors of Spanish dungeons, man-eating sharks, and strait-jacketed prisoners had their purpose. They convinced a crime-weary populace that the government was putting the screws to the bad guys. And they were a threat to dangle over the heads of federal prisoners: Screw up one more time and you're going to Alcatraz.

"The government has provided a place to tame tough guys like you," the warden of Leavenworth prison tells gangster Gat Brady in the Warner Brothers picture *Alcatraz Island*. "They take away his good time and transfer him to 'The Rock.'"

A view along "Broadway" (the corridor between B- and C Block), taken during a press tour in mid-August 1934, just days before the first shipment of new inmates arrived from McNeil Island, Washington. The guard is dressed in the old-style correctional officer's uniform, complete with optional bow-tie, which was worn when the penitentiary first opened. *(Photo courtesy San Francisco History Center, San Francisco Public Library, AAC-9368)*

AN INSIDE LOOK
The First Alcatraz Movies

Alcatraz Island arrived in theaters in 1937, three years after the opening of the federal prison for which it was named. It

Convicts lined up in the exercise yard for work details following the noontime meal. Work was a privilege on Alcatraz, and it was earned through good behavior. Men choosing not to work—or considered not trustworthy—spent up to 23 hours a day in their cells. *(Photo courtesy Golden Gate National Recreation Area, Park Archives, 82-C-17)*

was one of two Alcatraz-themed movies to be released that year; the other, *The Last Gangster,* was a somber morality tale starring Edward G. Robinson and Jimmy Stewart. *Alcatraz Island* was lighter fare, with a plot that seemed to exist largely for the purpose of showcasing the famous prison. Studio publicists promised an inside look at what they called "the prison fortress all gangland dreads." The movie "shows the prison formalities of signing in at the institution, scenes of the mess hall and prison yard," the *San Francisco Chronicle* told its readers. These were big selling points for an audience who could see the outside of the prison, but not the inside.

The film tells the story of Gat Brady, a good-hearted and non-violent gangster who is wrongly accused of murdering another inmate while serving time at Alcatraz. While it is by no measure an enduring piece of cinematic artistry, the movie does have the distinction of having coined many of the conventions that would define Alcatraz movies into the next century: the scene in which the arriving con learns how different Alcatraz is from other prisons, the interview with the warden, the speech from a longtime inmate who tells the new arrival that Alcatraz has broken many a weaker man. "Wait til you get in your bunk tonight," a fellow con tells Brady after he arrives at Alcatraz. "The fog settles in over the Bay and the siren in the lighthouse begins to moan. It's just the same in here as being in your grave—only you miss the fun of being dead."

Hollywood scriptwriters didn't have any more access to Alcatraz than did the tourists peering through telescopes on Fisherman's Wharf, but the movie's scriptwriters had clearly sifted through newspaper and magazine articles in search of Alcatraz lore. "A mechanical stool pigeon, how do you like that?" the newly arrived Brady remarks as he passes through the prison's metal detectors. An inmate in front of him fills him in on what to expect from the rest of the prison:

"These screws are poison. Handpicked from other federal stirs. They get three months schoolin' in McNeil's Island: target practice, scientific friskin', jujitsu, and readin' codes."

"Treat 'em like soldiers, eh?" Gat replies.

Armed correctional officers patrolled a network of guard towers, gun galleries, and catwalks that allowed them to observe virtually every corner of the prison—when they were manned. As the penitentiary aged, fewer and fewer guards were posted at night, a policy that was partially responsible for the success of the infamous Anglin–Morris escape in June 1962. *(Photo courtesy San Francisco History Center, San Francisco Public Library, AAC-9391)*

"They're as hard-boiled as G-men."

The exchange, along with several others in the film, is lifted almost verbatim from an article about Alcatraz that had appeared in the *Saturday Evening Post* the previous year.

Like Gat Brady, Joe Krozak (Edward G. Robinson), the protagonist of *The Last Gangster*, comes to the Rock after being convicted of income tax evasion, and like Brady, he learns quickly that the Rock isn't any old hoosegow. Krozak is a swaggering, self-centered big shot who idolizes Napoleon. During the long train ride to prison, we see him mouthing off

Correctional officers whose duties brought them in immediate contact with convicts, such as patrolling the cellhouse floor, went unarmed. Many guards, however, carried unauthorized (but effective) lead-weighted "saps" for close-in fighting. *(Photo courtesy Golden Gate National Recreation Area, Park Archives, GOGA-2316, 87-C-19)*

Convicts entering the Alcatraz mess hall, 1955. For many years, convicts sat at the 10-man tables visible in the background. *(Photo courtesy Golden Gate National Recreation Area, Park Archives, 82-C-4)*

Hollywood's interpretation of the mess hall in *The Last Gangster*. Many of the props are accurate for Alcatraz, such as the tin cups, coffee urn, and the compartmented trays, but the convicts' registry numbers are wildly exaggerated. The highest number issued at Alcatraz was 1,576. *(MGM, 1937; photo courtesy Everett Collection)*

to the other convict passengers. None of the cons know where they're headed—the shades have been drawn for the entire journey—and a pall settles over them when they feel a sudden rocking as their train is loaded onto a barge. The guards raise the shades and there in front of them is the gray outline of Alcatraz Island. "There she is, boys," one of the convicts sneers. "You're gonna snuggle in the arms of Alcatraz. If you ever hit a tougher stir it'll be when you step out of your coffin."

"Okay now," barks a guard. "You get five minutes more for conversation so you might as well get it out of your system. After that, you'll just be talking when you're told to."

But the inmates are all silent, ruminating over their fate.

Like *Alcatraz Island, The Last*

Gangster served as a kind of cinematic tour of Alcatraz, or of Alcatraz as Hollywood imagined it. We hear about the rule of silence and the limits on visitors, and visit the prison laundry, the mess hall with its row of menacing tear-gas canisters, and the hole. We're even treated to a prison riot, with tear-gas canisters erupting into plumes of smoke and choking convicts passing out in piles on the floor. There is really only one glaring departure from the bounds of realism. The film is set in 1927—seven years before Alcatraz opened.

The clothing issue room in the cellhouse basement was immediately adjacent to the shower room. Convicts were given a complete set of clothes, towels, and bedding on a weekly basis. *(Photo courtesy Golden Gate National Recreation Area, Park Archives, 77-C-394)*

A GENRE IS BORN

How to Make an Alcatraz Movie

TRAIN TO ALCATRAZ

A Republic Picture

5 Country of Origin U.S.A. 48-1121

Alcatraz Island and *The Last Gangster* relied on newspaper and magazine articles to get the skinny on Alcatraz, and those yellowed newspaper clippings are still a favorite source for Hollywood screenwriters who want to give their movies the imprimatur of authenticity. But over time, filmmakers have turned to another source for the lowdown on Alcatraz: previous movies. Since the release of those first two movies, conventions have grown up for the Alcatraz genre. It just wouldn't be an Alcatraz movie if someone didn't greet a new arrival with the phrase "Welcome to Alcatraz" or "Welcome to the Rock" or "Welcome to *La Isla De Los Alcatraces*" or even "Welcome to the Seaside Hotel." Nor would it be an Alcatraz movie if the movie's newly arrived inmate didn't have an initial meeting with the facility's heartless warden.

The purpose of these meetings is always to explain how Alcatraz will cow the most obdurate prisoner. "If you disobey the rules of society, they send you to prison," the warden tells Eastwood's Frank Morris in *Escape from Alcatraz*. "If you disobey the rules of prison, they send you to us. . . . We don't make good citizens, but we make excellent prisoners."

Over time, movie wardens became increasingly sadistic, and their introductory speeches increasingly overwrought. "You are among the selected sinners the state has decided should simmer in scum," an overly alliterative associate warden played by Gary Oldman tells inmate Henry Young (Kevin Bacon) in *Murder in the First* just before slicing his Achilles tendon with a razor blade. In the 1940s, BOP Director James Bennett had issued a strongly worded statement about coverage of the real-life Henry Young case, but this was the first movie to prompt the Bureau of Prisons to make a public statement about Hollywood's portrayal of Alcatraz. The Bureau issued a point-by-point refutation of the film's depiction of the prison as a barbaric torture chamber, taking particular

Kevin Bacon as Henry Young in *Murder in the First*. This studio photo includes one of the few details about Alcatraz that Hollywood depicted correctly: Young's registry number. *(Warner Brothers, 1995; photo courtesy Everett Collection)*

USP Alcatraz's first warden, James A. Johnston, described Henry Young (above) as an "alert, shrewd, intelligent, cunning, conspiring criminal with the exhibitionist's desire to dramatize his position and relate his misdeeds." *(Photo and quote courtesy Michael Esslinger)*

issue with Oldman's character. "The evil prison officer is one of the oldest and least imaginative movie clichés, and one of the most misleading," the Bureau's statement concluded (see p. 85).

(see p. 85)

Just as the character of the warden has become increasingly overblown with each successive film, so has the recitation of the rules, another scene that has become de rigueur in Alcatraz prison movies.

The real rules were strict enough to impress the viewers of *Alcatraz Island*. "Are they on the level with that rule about cleaning your plate?" Gat Brady asks another con on his first trip to the mess hall. "Here, you got to eat your spinach and like it," the con replies. But contemporary audiences, raised on a steady diet of prime-time

The Alcatraz warden's office in 1963. This view, taken shortly after the penitentiary closed, shows the no-nonsense décor that included portraits of President John F. Kennedy and Attorney General Robert F. Kennedy. *(Photo courtesy Golden Gate National Recreation Area, Park Archives, 77-C-320)*

Hollywood's recreation of the same office in *Escape From Alcatraz*. In this case, the prop department nailed down the details of the warden's office almost exactly, right down to the warden's private doorway. The only criticism is that the set designers made the office almost look too nice. *(Paramount/Malpaso, 1979; photo courtesy Everett Collection)*

violence, are not likely to be impressed by cons being sent to their cells without supper. By the time *Murder in the First* hit the screen, the punishment for not cleaning your plate had been made a tad more severe. "You know the rules!" a guard bellows at Henry Young. "You don't eat, you go to solitary!"

Another stock scene in Alcatraz movies is the conversation between the new inmate and the hardened con, who explains that Alcatraz is the toughest prison of them all. "This is the last stop on the hardest line on the prison system," an inmate tells the young Clarence Carnes (Michael Beck)

Conspirators Miran Thompson (left), Clarence Carnes (center), and Sam Shockley (right) headed for trial in San Francisco following the deadly three-day "Battle of Alcatraz" in May 1946. This abortive escape has been portrayed in three movies: *Birdman of Alcatraz* (1962), *Alcatraz: The Whole Shocking Story* (1980), and *Six Against the Rock* (1987). *(Photo courtesy Golden Gate National Recreation Area, Park Archives, Don Denevi Collection, P83-166.11n)*

in the TV movie *Alcatraz: The Whole Shocking Story*. "You don't get here unless you're the worst—and that's how they treat you. You try to fight that you'll end up dead or crazy."

In truth, the worst terror on Alcatraz was the stultifying boredom, particularly in the early years when the rule of silence was strictly enforced. Unable to kill time boasting and telling stories, inmates had little to do but pace their cells and count the minutes until Saturday afternoons, when they would be allowed two hours of socializing in the Recreation Yard. Perhaps the best description of the soul-eating monotony of prison life comes from the 1962 film *The Birdman of Alcatraz*. "The routine's always the same," Burt Lancaster's Robert Stroud explains. "You sit and listen to your heartbeat. And you hear your life ticking away. The thing that swells in your head until you lose your mind is that you know, absolutely for sure, what's coming next."

The boredom helps to explain why Alcatraz inmates spent so much time hatching escape plots. Many had earned their visit to the Rock by sneaking out of other institutions, and figuring out how to break out of Alcatraz at least gave them a way to occupy their time. "When you're in prison, you have nothing else to do but think of one thing," observed Clint Eastwood, star of *Escape from Alcatraz* (1979). "It's amazing how creative they got." But while real and fictional Alcatraz escapes have provided plotlines for movies like *Escape from Alcatraz*, *Alcatraz: The Whole Shocking Story*, and *Alcatraz*

Breakout, the Rock's escape-proof reputation proved a bit of a challenge to filmmakers in the thirties and forties when Alcatraz was a popular cinematic setting.

Every American had heard that Alcatraz was impossible to escape from: there were the metal detectors; the barbed wire fences; the twelve or more daily head counts; the specially

trained guards; and, most formidable of all, the cold and treacherous waters of the bay. All the same, an escape-proof prison limits your story-telling options considerably, and Hollywood often found it convenient to make Alcatraz more permeable.

Escapes figured prominently in movies like *King of Alcatraz* (1938), in which an escaped Alcatraz inmate takes over a cruise ship; *San Francisco Docks* (1941), in which an escaped Alcatraz inmate commits a waterfront murder; and *Seven Miles from Alcatraz* (1942), in which two chicken-hearted Alcatraz inmates escape to a nearby lighthouse and wind up defeating a Nazi spy ring.

None of these movies cared to dwell on the question of just how the escape had been effected. "It's no cinch breaking out of the Rock, war or no war," Champ, the cowardly con in *Seven Miles from Alcatraz* explains in a coy voiceover, "and we're not going to tell you how we did it on account of that's a professional secret." In most of these movies, escaping from Alcatraz was a matter of jumping into the water and breast-stroking to shore. Steve Lowry, the lovelorn gangster played by George Raft in *House Across the Bay* (1940), learns his show-girl wife is two-timing him and breaks out of Alcatraz that evening, arriving at her Alameda nightclub in time to catch the second set. It's only after he realizes that she's better off without him that he returns to the water and lets himself be shot by a patrol boat. In the next scene we

hear two off-camera voices discussing Lowry's death. "What a sucker the guy was to try to escape from Alcatraz," one says. "No one'll ever make it."

TOUGH GUYS
The Changing Portrayal of Alcatraz Inmates

Alcatraz was supposed to be a place for the nation's worst criminals, although many were garden-variety thugs whose intractability had earned them a ticket to the Rock. Being sent to Alcatraz was supposed to teach them humility, but it also gave them a certain cachet.

"They tell me the government is going to put a swimming pool in on the Rock," one Alcatraz-

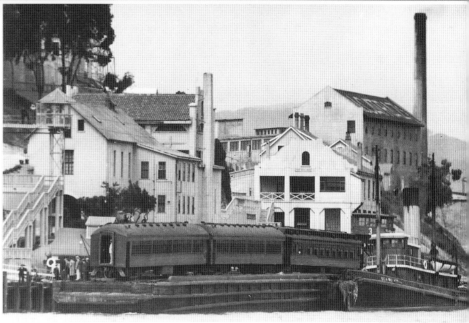

bound con remarks to another in the noir flick *Prison Train* (1938).

"Oh yeah?"

"Yeah. And why shouldn't they? They're catering to a better class of people."

This "better class of people" was, of course, tailor-made for Hollywood drama—risk-taking bad boys, who talked tough and bowed down to no one. But the Hays Production Code of 1930 stipulated that "the sympathy of the audience should never be thrown to the side of crime, wrongdoing, evil, or sin." Gangsters were the glamour boys of the era, but they were not supposed to be glamorized.

The Code guaranteed that Steve Lowry, the gangster-inmate in *House Across the Bay*, would meet an untimely end and lose the affections of his beautiful wife, Brenda. Brenda means to be faithful to Lowry, renting an apartment with a view of Alcatraz so she can feel close to him after he's sent to prison. Returning from her first visit to the island, she befriends the other "Rock Widows" on the boat and discovers that to them, she's "just another Jenny with a Johnny on the Rock." One of them reminds Brenda not to get too sentimental about her

The first large transfer of prisoners to Alcatraz was a trainload of 53 inmates from the federal penitentiary in Atlanta; the men arrived on August 22, 1934. The train cars were loaded onto a railroad barge at Tiburon, and a tug towed the barge to the island dock. Prison officials, concerned about escape attempts, took numerous security precautions. (*Photo courtesy Golden Gate National Recreation Area, Park Archives, 75-C-46*)

convicted spouse. "Your guy's so smart he didn't have the sense to go straight," she cautions. Before long, Brenda's being romanced by a handsome airplane designer, who takes her for a lofty spin over the very island where her husband is incarcerated. "Look, you can see Alcatraz," he says. "Now some of those poor devils down there would envy us up here—free! Free to go wherever we care to."

Joe Krozac, the arrogant mobster from *The Last Gangster,* will also lose his gal to a more upstanding fellow. When his foreign wife finally learns enough English to understand that he's a cold-blooded killer, she divorces him and remarries a clean-cut reporter played by Jimmy Stewart, who raises Krozac's son as his own. Krozac winds up gunned down in a dark alley after being released from prison, abandoned both by his family and by the members of his former gang.

Some film gangsters did have the sense to go straight, and thus live long enough to see the credits roll. Gat Brady, the hero of *Alcatraz Island,* is reformed by his stay in Alcatraz. "I used to think dough was the most important thing in the world," he muses on his release. Champ and Jimbo, the unpatriotic criminals in *Seven Miles from Alcatraz,* have also turned over a new leaf by the movie's end, realizing that even crooks have to join the fight against Hitler. "We're hoodlums," Jimbo explains, "but we're American hoodlums."

IN THE law-and-order atmosphere of the fifties, criminals, reformed or not, were no longer the protagonists of Alcatraz films, they were the villains. Alcatraz was portrayed as a heroic institution, a triumph of society over criminal elements. In the atomic-age thriller *Experiment Alcatraz* (1959), a select group of Alcatraz inmates receive a get-out-of-jail-free card in exchange for agreeing to be injected with a radioactive substance that might be the cure for "a rare blood disease." When one of the prisoners murders another and blames his act of violence on the injection, it is up to the movie's physician hero to prove that the inmate committed the murder for his own nefarious purposes. The message of the film: Let the crooks out of Alcatraz and they'll do nothing but cause trouble.

But by the end of the 1950s,

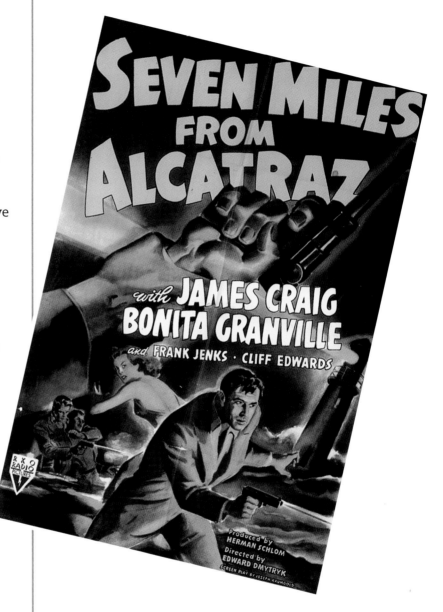

Robert Stroud in a mug shot made in 1952 while serving time at Alcatraz. The nickname "Birdman of Alcatraz" did not come into use until 1955, when author Tom Gaddis coined the title for his semi-biographical book about Stroud's life. *(Photo courtesy Golden Gate National Recreation Area, Park Archives, 87-C-15)*

things were beginning to change in Hollywood. The Production Code Administration Office had lost much of its power to regulate movie content, as had the House Un-American Activities Committee. Hollywood, reveling in this newfound freedom, began making movies that challenged conventional thinking about American institutions. One of these institutions was Alcatraz. In 1962, United Artists released *Birdman of Alcatraz,* a drama-cum-polemic starring Burt Lancaster as Alcatraz inmate Robert Stroud.

Inside Alcatraz, the inmates and guards knew Stroud as a violent, brilliant, and arrogant troublemaker who had killed two men without showing a shred of remorse. But outside Alcatraz, Stroud was a symbol of the redemptive powers of the human soul—a man with a third-grade education who was popularly perceived to have used his time in prison to become an expert on bird diseases, a man whose quest for dignity was thwarted by the prison system's obsession with conformity. "You'll conform to our ideas of how you should behave," Warden Harvey Shoemaker (Karl Malden) tells Stroud early in the movie. But Stroud refuses to conform. "I won't lick your hand and that's what eats you, ain't it, keeper?"

THE FEDERAL government had come to expect that Hollywood would treat its most famous prison with respect, and federal Bureau of Prison officials knew how to make their displeasure

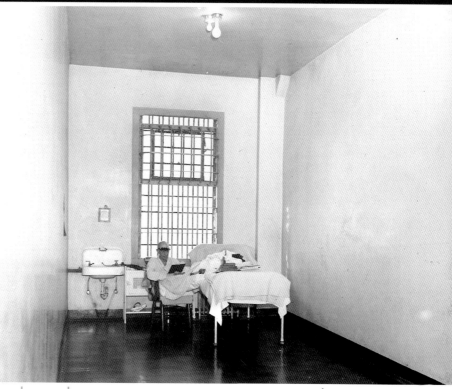

felt when the film industry didn't comply. Desilu Production's television series, *The Untouchables*, was a law-and-order show that portrayed heroic federal G-man Elliott Ness cracking down on gangsters and racketeers. But when *The Big Train*, a 1961 two-part episode about gangster Al Capone's transfer to Alcatraz, showed Capone bribing prison guards at the Atlanta federal

During his last eleven years on the island, Stroud was confined to a converted ward in the prison's hospital, ostensibly because of ongoing medical problems. Stroud used the bed near the window as a table for his books and papers. He slept in a second bed next to the entrance to cell. *(Photo courtesy Golden Gate National Recreation Area, Park Archives, Ordway Collection, GOGA-3249)*

DEPARTMENT OF JUSTICE, BUREAU OF INVESTIGATION
IDENTIFICATION DIVISION, WASHINGTON, D. C.

Al Capone's official mug shot (above), taken when he first went into federal custody for income tax evasion, and an earlier portrait (right), taken while he was still boss of Chicago's bootlegging and prostitution rackets. The scar along his left cheek that gave Capone his nickname is clearly visible in the latter photo. *(Photos courtesy Golden Gate National Recreation Area, Park Archives)*

penitentiary, BOP Director James Bennett was reportedly so incensed that he threatened to have the licenses of ten ABC affiliates revoked if they aired the second half of the show. The show aired anyway, but with a disclaimer: "Nothing herein is intended to reflect unfavorably on the courageous and responsible prison guards who supervised Al Capone during his internment in the Federal Penitentiary in Atlanta, and during his transfer from Atlanta to Alcatraz."

Filmmakers had been interested in making a movie about Stroud since the late forties, but the Bureau of Prisons had always managed to deflect their curiosity. Some have speculated that Hollywood's interest in Stroud contributed to Alcatraz Warden Edwin B. Swope's decision to transfer a perfectly healthy Stroud to the prison hospital, where he would spend eleven years isolated from other prisoners. Twentieth Century Fox talked about making a Stroud movie in 1958, but was reportedly dissuaded by the Bureau of Prisons. It was only when Lancaster made Stroud a personal project that the idea got off the ground, this time at United Artists.

For Lancaster, the lesson of *Birdman of Alcatraz* was that "the initial concept of prisons—to send men away to be punished—is not only inhuman but outdated and outmoded." Up to this point, Alcatraz movies had never questioned the prison's *raison d'etre*. Swaggering gangsters had to learn to play by society's rules, and the first step was to teach them that they weren't as special as they thought they were. *The Big Train* culminates with a cocky Al Capone being booked into Alcatraz. "You know my name—everybody knows my name," he tells the guard who signs him in. But there are no celebrities at Alcatraz, and a chastened Capone has to spell his first and last names, one letter at a time, just like every other con. *The Last Gangster*'s Joe Krozac also gets his comeuppance. Soon after he arrives, the warden calls him into his office to tell him that his wife has given birth to a son. Krozac demands to use the prison telephone. The warden refuses.

"Now look here, little man," Krozac bellows. "I've had enough of this. . . . This is Joe Krozac. You ain't talking to any jumped-up sucker that knocked over a corner cigar store."

The warden is unimpressed. "Now let's get that straight," he tells Krozac in a bored voice. "I'm talking to #8429. . . . And if #8429 isn't a good boy, he won't see anybody, for a long time."

But in *Birdman of Alcatraz,* reducing men to numbers isn't the cure, it's the disease. Alcatraz is the embodiment of a rigid, compassionless, soul-crushing system that strips the humanity from all but a few who have the strength to resist. Near the end of the movie, Stroud meets again with Harvey Shoemaker, who is now the warden of Alcatraz. Shoemaker has confiscated Stroud's critique of the penal system, telling Stroud that he has yet to show a single sign of rehabilitation. Stroud challenges him to define the term, explain-ing that his dictionary says it means "to invest again with dignity."

"Do you consider that part of your job, Harvey, to give a man back the dignity he once had? You want your prisoners to dance out the gates like puppets on a string with rubber-stamp values impressed by you. With your sense of conformity, your sense of behavior, even your sense of morality. That's why you're a failure, Harvey, you and the entire science of penology. You rob prisoners of the most important thing in their lives: their individuality."

Just as Lancaster hoped, the movie inspired in an enormous outpouring of support for the still-incarcerated Stroud. Movie reviewers urged viewers to write letters to Attorney General Robert Kennedy demanding

Stroud's release, and supporters gathered tens of thousands of signatures at tables in front of the movie theaters. The campaign was ultimately unsuccessful—Stroud died a year later at the Medical Center for Federal Prisoners in Springfield, Missouri—but it did signal a sea change in public feeling about prisons, and particularly about Alcatraz. People no longer thrilled to rumors of the torments allegedly experienced on the Rock. They wanted to hear about people who had regained their dignity by fighting the Rock and winning.

Alcatraz was closed in 1963, less than a year after the release of *Birdman of Alcatraz*. Closure was inevitable as the deteriorating prison grew increasingly

INSIDE THE ROCK CALLED ALCATRAZ THEY TRIED TO CHAIN A VOLCANO THEY CALLED 'THE BIRD MAN'!

HAROLD HECHT PRESENTS
BURT LANCASTER

BIRD MAN OF ALCATRAZ

KARL MALDEN / THELMA RITTER / NEVILLE BRAND
EDMOND O'BRIEN
with BETTY FIELD TELLY SAVALAS GUY TROSPER
screenplay by GUY TROSPER based on the book by TOM GADDIS
directed by JOHN FRANKENHEIMER
produced by STUART MILLAR and GUY TROSPER
music ELMER BERNSTEIN
A NORMA PRODUCTION
released thru UNITED ARTISTS

Convicts boarding the island launch on the morning of the penitentiary's closing, March 21, 1963. The last prisoner to leave was Frankie Weatherman, a bank robber, whose ungrammatical final comment would serve as an epitaph of sorts: "Alcatraz was never no good for nobody." *(Photo courtesy Golden Gate National Recreation Area, Park Archives, Don Denevi Collection, P83-144.D67n)*

expensive to maintain, but it was also true that the prison's harsh image no longer jibed with contemporary ideas about crime and punishment. "Let us reject the spirit of retribution and attempt to balance the need of deterrence with the possibility of rehabilitation," Attorney General Robert F. Kennedy said when he announced that Alcatraz would be closing.

In the language of cinema, Alcatraz was now the steel boot of the system, a place where human dignity was crushed by rigid and sadistic conformity. When Clint Eastwood's Frank Morris arrives on the Rock in *Escape from Alcatraz*, he encounters an institution where an elderly inmate is driven to cut off his own fingers with a hatchet after the warden seizes the paints, canvases, and brushes that made prison life bearable. Eastwood's escape isn't just a prison break, it's a blow against the system. The last scene of the movie shows the prison's warden finding a flower from Alcatraz on nearby Angel Island; the flower's presence indicates that the three escaped convicts have made it to dry land. "They drowned," the warden insists, ripping the flower into shreds. But the audience knows his gesture is futile. After all, the movie tells us, Alcatraz closed less than a year later. Frank Morris and the Anglin brothers struck a blow not just for freedom, but for Freedom.

In the movies, the blow will be struck again and again. Long after Alcatraz ceased to function

As institutional rules were loosened, Alcatraz inmates came to enjoy privileges unimaginable during the early years of the institution. Painting, musical instruments, and even knitting were popular pastimes. This 1956 view of a fledgling artist's cell shows the amount of energy some men devoted to their hobbies. *(Photo courtesy Sun Francisco History Center, San Francisco Public Library, AAC-9343)*

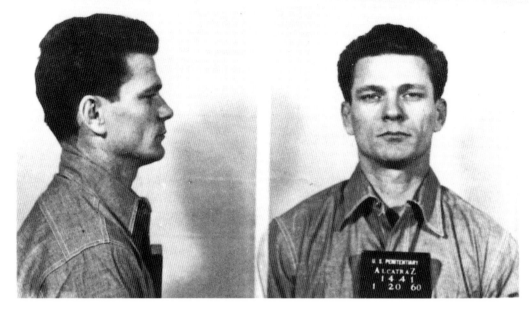

The real Frank Lee Morris in his 1960 Alcatraz mug shot *(top, photo courtesy Golden Gate National Recreation Area, Park Archives, GOGA 82-C-6)*, and as portrayed by Clint Eastwood in *Escape from Alcatraz (bottom, Paramount/ Malpaso, 1976; photo courtesy Everett Collection)*

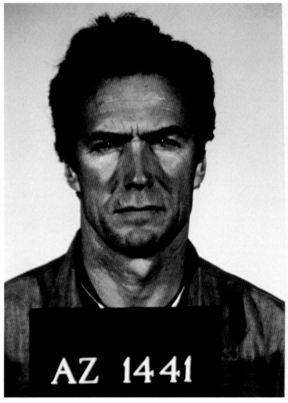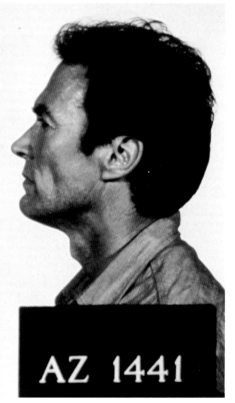

as a prison, filmmakers have continued to battle its alleged injustices. In *Murder in the First,* Kevin Bacon's Henry Young has been reduced to a trembling, crippled wreck by a three-year stay in the Alcatraz dungeons. After he kills another inmate, Rufus McCain, a young lawyer convinces him to try a new defense: "Devil's Island made me do it." The two men put Alcatraz on trial and a jury finds the institution "guilty of crimes against humanity."

Today, most people who are familiar with contemporary maximum-security prisons say that violence, overcrowding, and gang activity make them much scarier places to be than Alcatraz ever was. Still, Alcatraz visitors often comment that "They should make more prisons like this today." The Steven Seagal vehicle *Half Past Dead* uses this sentiment as a premise; in the movie, Alcatraz has been reopened, this time with an on-site execution chamber. The movie revives the conventions of previous Alcatraz films: there's a welcoming speech by the warden, the warning about the impossibility of escape, the tour of the high-tech gizmos keeping the prisoners in line. But this movie doesn't ask us to condemn Alcatraz. "Alcatraz is a bad place for bad people," a Bureau of Prisons official played by Morris Chestnut explains near the start of the film. "If there's any discomfort behind these walls, well, that's how it should be." The language has been updated, but the sentiment could just as easily have been expressed in 1937.

THE GATES OF HELL
Alcatraz as Metaphor

Throughout its time as a prison, both scriptwriters and journalists likened a stay on the Rock to a season in hell, both because of the torments allegedly endured there, and because these torments were supposed to have been earned by the convicts' bad behavior. In 1958, *San Francisco Examiner* columnist Robert Ruark wrote an article arguing that if Alcatraz should close —a possibility that had been discussed regularly since 1934—it should be kept as "a kind of national shrine against wrongdoing." "As a moral it is as simple as the concept of heaven and hell," he wrote. "The good go to San Francisco, the bad to Alcatraz . . . "

Ruark would get his wish. Alcatraz became a National Historic Landmark and part of the national park system in 1972, and if anything, the association between the island and Satan's kingdom has only become more pronounced in the intervening years. Nearly every film set on a post-prison Alcatraz involves the protagonists being chased around the deserted facility by a crazed killer, a terrorist, or even by Satan himself. A recurring theme is that the island is home to evil spirits or some other kind of bad ju-ju—a literal interpretation of the term "Hellcatraz." "Is it possible that spirits from Alcatraz prison's evil past can still be held captive after all these years?" asks the cover copy on

the direct-to-video release *Force of Darkness* (1987), a film that situates the literal Gates of Hell somewhere in cellblock C.

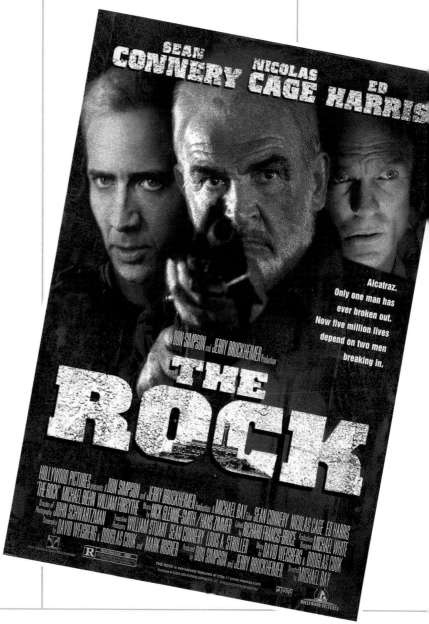

Hollywood constructed a replica guard tower on Alcatraz for the 1976 production *The Enforcer (left, photo courtesy John Cantwell Collection, Guy Washington, photographer)*, modeling it after the island's original Dock Tower *(below, photo courtesy Golden Gate National Recreation Area, Park Archives, Mary Bowman Collection, P83-161.4n)*. The replica tower is blown up in the movie's finale. In a backhanded compliment to the set directors' talents, at least one historian protested that the National Park Service had allowed the film crew to destroy an authentic guard tower.

The first post-prison movie to use Alcatraz as a location was *Point Blank,* a 1967 noir thriller starring Lee Marvin and directed by John Boorman. The film begins when Marvin, as a free-lance robber named Walker, wakes up in an Alcatraz cell where he's been shot and left for dead after being double-crossed during a heist. He somehow manages to swim to shore and then begins the process of trying to track down those responsible and regain his share of the take. But it's never entirely clear whether Walker's surreal adventures are real, or the feverish imaginings of a dying man as he descends into a hell of his own making. "You died on Alcatraz, all right," one character tells him.

Point Blank was followed by *The Enforcer* (1976), in which Clint Eastwood's Dirty Harry has to chase down a bunch of terrorists who have holed up on Alcatraz—a plot that would be redeployed in *The Rock* (1996), with the addition of poison-gas missiles, underground tunnels, and some cool special effects. *The Enforcer* alerted film-makers to the spooky allure of playing cat-and-mouse in the deserted cellhouse. If the movies are to be believed, San Francisco residents are constantly climbing into boats and voyaging over to Alcatraz in the middle of the night without telling anyone where they're going. Once on the island, they

Though the screenwriter invented some of *The Rock's* settings—such as the maze of tunnels through which Sean Connery and Nicolas Cage accessed the island—others actually exist and can be seen by today's visitors. Here, Connery and Cage stand in front of the wire-mesh walls that once protected the cellhouse library. *(Hollywood Pictures, 1996; photo courtesy Everett Collection)*

The corridor in front of A Block was a tight fit for those involved in the filming of this scene from *So I Married an Axe Murderer*. The dolly shot, with its associated track, camera, lights, cables, and reflectors, crowds the corridor, leaving little room for cast and crew members to maneuver. *(Photo by and courtesy Warren White)*

might encounter a psychopath boyfriend *(Kicks)*, a voracious demon *(Slaughterhouse Rock, Force of Darkness)*, or former Alcatraz inmate Frank Morris *(Terror on Alcatraz)*. Regardless, you know some bodies are going to pile up before sunrise.

In many of these movies, the victims are hapless tourists who come to Alcatraz cracking jokes and snapping pictures only to discover that a sinister force still lurks. Tourists are locked up in cells in *The Rock,* terrified by inexplicable happenings in *Force of Darkness,* and massacred by the boatload in *Slaughterhouse Rock* and *Terror on Alcatraz.* "Alcatraz has become a tourist attraction?" former inmate John Patrick Mason (Sean Connery) asks in *The Rock.* Given the apparent risks, you understand his surprise.

ALCATRAZ AND HOLLYWOOD
A Symbiotic Relationship

Tourism is one of the challenges filmmakers face when they come to Alcatraz, which might account for the shabby treatment tourists receive in the movies. The National Park Service requires that the island be kept open to visitors during filming, so there's always the risk that a scene supposedly set in 1941 might have a guy wearing an Ozzy Osbourne t-shirt walking through the background. During the filming of *Escape from Alcatraz*, Paramount Pictures dealt with that problem by buying up all the boat tickets for the days they planned to shoot.

As an example of the lengths to which Hollywood will go to achieve the desired lighting effects, this maze of cables, support brackets, and floodlights was installed on the roof and aimed down through the skylights to illuminate the inside the cellhouse for the shooting of *The Rock*. *(Photo courtesy John Cantwell Collection)*

The National Park Service no longer allows filmmakers to do that, which means that movie crews have to find ways to work around the island's visitors. In the early days of the park, when there were fewer visitors, that sometimes meant carrying on as though the tourists weren't there at all. Ranger Rich Weideman recalls a chase scene for the movie *Kicks* being filmed in the cellhouse while tours cycled in and out, unfazed, apparently, by the rounds of blanks being fired around them. More recent filmmakers have simply cordoned off the spectators if they couldn't complete their filming before the tourists arrived or after they'd gone home. That can provide visitors with some unexpected

The northern tip of Alcatraz served as the island's industrial area when the penitentiary was in operation. These factory buildings are now closed to the public, and movie crews frequently use their large empty interiors for set construction shops, dressing rooms, food service, and other myriad activities that support the filming. *(Photo by and courtesy Roy Eisenhardt)*

thrills. Alcatraz rangers tell the story of the time Sean Connery, on the island while filming *The Rock*, arrived at the dock just as visitors were lining up for the last boat to the mainland. "Sean! Sean!" a woman began yelling. "You're the love of my life!" To which her astonished ten-year-old son replied, "But *Mom*, what about Dad?"

Tourists aren't the only challenge Alcatraz poses for filmmakers. There is the weather, which is unpredictable and often chilling; the historic buildings, which have to be treated with care; and the island's birds, who must not be disturbed by lights and noise during their seven-month nesting season. The grounds are littered with so much rusty metal that actor Nicolas Cage dubbed the place "Tetanus World" during his time shooting *The Rock*. And all the supplies—trailers, vehicles, film equipment, even food and water—have to be brought to the island by boat. Film companies even have to provide their own electricity, as the island doesn't have enough power to support a major movie shoot. All in all, filming a scene on the island costs about three times as much as it would to shoot the same scene on the mainland.

What keeps filmmakers coming back is that there is simply no other place like it. The cellhouse can be reproduced in Culver City, but not the views of San Francisco or the prison's grim, gray profile. "There's a presence the island has that cannot be recreated in a studio," Ranger Craig Glassner observes. "To be out there when the fog is roaring in across the bay under

The crew of *Escape From Alcatraz* thought they were leaving a present for the National Park Service when they painted this 15-foot mural in the lower entrance to the prison. Flanking the "Welcome" sign (but not shown here) were equally large paintings of the Department of the Interior insignia and the NPS arrowhead emblem. All three murals were painted out within a week of their creation. *(Photo by and courtesy John Martini)*

The main aisle through the cellhouse, known as Broadway, has appeared in every movie shot on the Rock. Since Alcatraz opened to the public in 1973, all of the ground floor cells along Broadway have been repainted by various production companies and refurnished with prop beds, linens, and personal items. *(Courtesy Golden Gate National Recreation Area, Park Archives, Betty Wallar Collection, P83-170.152)*

the Golden Gate. To be out there at night when the night herons are hunting. Place has a certain power—just reading about it or seeing pictures doesn't have the same effect. And I think Hollywood has come to realize that."

Nearly every part of Alcatraz contains a souvenir of Hollywood's many visits. In the basement of the cellhouse, for instance, you can see the faint remnants of a mural painted on a corridor wall by the crew of *Escape from Alcatraz*. The mural, created as a surprise gift to the island's staff, was bordered by sprocket holes, like a frame of 35 mm film. It said "Welcome to Alcatraz," and was signed by many members of the film's cast and crew, including Clint Eastwood. The National Park Service wasn't as touched by the gift as

the film crew had hoped; it was painted over almost as soon as it was unveiled.

Many other traces of the film remain, however, including the

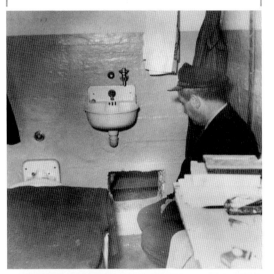

June 12, 1962: An officer stares at the hole carved through the back of the cell once occupied by Frank Lee Morris. *(Photo courtesy San Francisco History Center, San Francisco Public Library, AAC-9561)* Clint Eastwood (below), portraying Frank Lee Morris in *Escape from Alcatraz*, reenacts the moment when Morris began chipping away the concrete surrounding the air vent in the back of his cell. *(Paramount/Malpaso, 1979; photo courtesy Everett Collection)*

The aisle between C Block and the blank rear wall of D Block (left) was nicknamed "Park Place" and "Seedy (C-D) Street." Many convicts preferred the cells along this aisle, especially on the upper tiers facing the blank wall, which provided a degree of privacy but didn't distract them with views of the city and its unattainable attractions. *(Photo courtesy San Francisco History Center, San Francisco Public Library, AAC-9371)*

yellow lines that are still visible running down Broadway. No such lines existed in the prison era and so they were supposed to be painted with removable paint. As it happened, the "removable" paint has lasted longer than many of the prison's other paint jobs, withstanding more than two decades of trampling. *The Escape from Alcatraz* crew also received permission to jackhammer holes in the back of several cells to simulate the holes made by the escaping prisoners. National Park Service officials didn't want the actual escape cells altered, so the film crew used other cells, which still have the holes in them today.

Other movies have left their signature on the cellhouse as well, which is why the building resembles the Winchester Mystery House in places, with portions restored to different eras and with varying degrees of accuracy. Take a close look at the cell numbers in C-Block for instance. The numbers on the cells that were used to hold hostages during the 1946 uprising were repainted during the filming of the 1987 television movie *Six Against the Rock*. Unfortunately, the numbers they painted aren't exactly right—the cell numbered 403 is actually cell number 404, and so on. Another odd phenomenon is the visitation area, a cold concrete room that seems unchanged from the 1930s. In actuality, the room was remodeled to be more hospitable

in the mid-fifties. Prison officials added wood paneling, wall-to-wall carpeting, a suspended acoustic ceiling, and a wash-room. The cozy decor wasn't exactly the look the makers of *Murder in the First* had in mind though, so they restored the visitation area to the bare concrete room it had been when the prison first opened.

These days the NPS is more strict about changes to prison buildings. Any change to the island's physical structure, even hammering a nail into a wall, requires explicit permission. The National Park Service has been working on a plan to restore the building to a single era, probably the early 1960s, to redress the hodgepodge of different time periods you see in the building now.

But while some of Hollywood's past alterations are regrettable, there's no doubt that if it weren't for Hollywood, the prison would look far shabbier than it does. *Escape from Alcatraz* brought fresh coats of paint to the kitchen and D-Block, and *Six Against the Rock* recreated the control center and repainted some of the cells in C-Block. *Alcatraz: The Whole Shocking Story* paid for the refurbishing of staff offices in the old dock-level barracks (Building 64), while *Murder in the First* funded the restoration of a guard tower on the dock and *The Rock* paid for the removal of eighty 55-gallon drums of hazardous waste.

Hollywood has also provided many of the details that give visitors a sense of what the penitentiary was like when it was open. Most of what you see in the cells, for instance, are movie props: The cots and many of the toilets are from *Escape from Alcatraz*; the pillows are from *Murder in the First*; and many of the bookshelves were built for *Alcatraz: The Whole Shocking Story*.

The dining room is also largely furnished by Hollywood, including the metal detectors outside the room and the menu board *(Escape from Alcatraz)* and the benches *(Murder in the First)*. The control center by the visitor's viewing area is a Hollywood set that was built for *Six Against the Rock*, using historical photos as references. And the signs outside the hospital and the visiting area are leftovers from *Murder in*

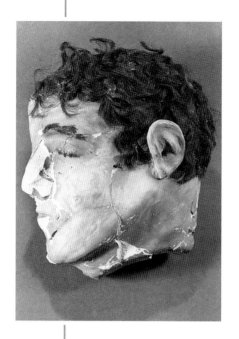

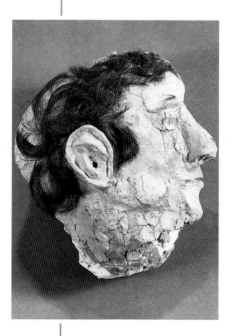

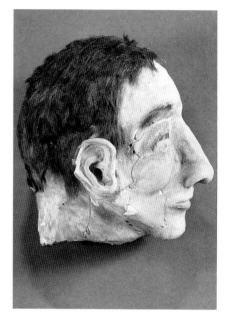

The original dummy heads made by Frank Morris and John and Clarence Anglin to deceive the Alcatraz guards are now in the collection of the National Park Service. The heads' construction materials include soap, plaster, concrete, human hair, paint, and coiled electrical cords. The National Park Service feels the heads are too fragile to be exhibited on the island. Instead, replica heads (created for the *America's Most Wanted* television program) are displayed in the escape cells. *(Courtesy Golden Gate National Recreation Area, Park Archives, P85-060.4/.5/.6)*

the First. If you look closely, you can see that they are cardboard.

Even some of the artifacts on display were originally Hollywood props. When the television show *America's Most Wanted* came to the island to do an episode about the 1962 escape, they furnished the actual escape cells with fake air vents and made reproductions of the dummy heads and jury-rigged tools used by Frank Morris and the Anglin brothers. The real dummy heads are too fragile to handle or display, but the Hollywood replicas are accurate enough give the island's visitors a sense of how the famed escape took place. It seems that the Rock needs Hollywood almost as much as Hollywood needs the Rock.

Hollywood and the National Park Service have different mis-sions, of course. Hollywood is in the business of telling stories, whether or not they are true. For Hollywood, Alcatraz will always be a place of mystery and foreboding, a dark castle filled with hardened cons, cruel wardens, desperate killers, and malicious spirits. The real Alcatraz is far more complex. But that doesn't mean Hollywood's version has nothing to teach us. Hollywood's Alcatraz is a reflection of our own fears and obsessions, our ambivalent feelings about crime and punishment, and our urge to give evil a permanent address. Its images and stories are like the fog that veils the island for much of the year. They may keep us from getting a clear view, but they are as intrinsic to the island's history as the tides.

Alcatraz today, as viewed from the Golden Gate Bridge. The National Park Service opened the island to the public for the first time in 1973, and it has now been a historic site for longer than it served as a penitentiary. However, in the minds of American moviegoers, the name "Alcatraz" will always evoke the 29 years—1934 to 1963—during which the Rock housed America's most notorious prisoners. *(Photo by and courtesy Brenda Tharp)*

Starring Alcatraz

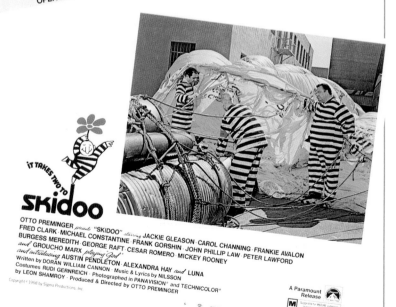

"No one has ever escaped from Alcatraz...and no one ever will."

CLINT EASTWOOD
ESCAPE FROM ALCATRAZ

PARAMOUNT PICTURES Presents a MALPASO Company/SIEGEL Film Co-Starring PATRICK McGOOHAN · Executive Producer ROBERT DALEY · Screenplay by RICHARD TUGGLE
Based on the Book by J. CAMPBELL BRUCE · Music by JERRY FIELDING · Produced and Directed by DON SIEGEL · A PARAMOUNT PICTURE

OPENS FRIDAY, JUNE 22nd AT A THEATRE NEAR YOU.

IT TAKES TWO TO
SKiDOO

OTTO PREMINGER *presents* "SKIDOO" *starring* JACKIE GLEASON · CAROL CHANNING · FRANKIE AVALON
FRED CLARK · MICHAEL CONSTANTINE · FRANK GORSHIN · JOHN PHILLIP LAW · PETER LAWFORD
BURGESS MEREDITH · GEORGE RAFT · CESAR ROMERO · MICKEY ROONEY
and GROUCHO MARX *playing God* · *and introducing* AUSTIN PENDLETON · ALEXANDRA HAY *and* LUNA
Written by DORAN WILLIAM CANNON · Music & Lyrics by NILSSON
Costumes RUDI GERNREICH · Photographed in PANAVISION® and TECHNICOLOR®
by LEON SHAMROY · Produced & Directed by OTTO PREMINGER
Copyright© 1968 by Sigma Productions, Inc.

A Paramount
Release

A MAN walks into a prison.
That's the premise of the more
than two dozen Alcatraz movies
made between 1937 and the
present. The Alcatraz of these
films may be the notorious dungeon, the decrepit building, or
the sensational tourist attraction, but it is always a spooky,
sinister place. Here are the
movies that helped make Alcatraz famous—the blockbusters,
the classics, the forgotten films
noir, and the direct-to-video
releases. In some of these
movies, Alcatraz is the star of
the show, in others, the island
is a shadowy figure lurking
in the background. In each of
them, however, it does its part
to perpetuate the island's sinister reputation.

Title: *The Last Gangster,* directed by Edward Ludwig

Starring: Edward G. Robinson, James Stewart, Rose Stradner, Douglas Scott

Year: 1937 (MGM)

Plot: A gangster (Edward G. Robinson) spends ten years at Alcatraz; when he gets out he finds he's lost his wife, his child, his money, and his gang.

Sample Dialogue: "There she is boys. You're gonna snuggle in the arms of Alcatraz. If you ever hit a tougher stir it'll be when you step out of your coffin."

Hollywood Touch: The movie is set in 1927. Alcatraz didn't open until 1934.

Film Title: *Alcatraz Island,* directed by William C. McGann

Starring: John Litel, Ann Sheridan, Mary Maguire

Year: 1937 (Warner Brothers)

Plot: Racketeer Gat Brady is sent to Alcatraz where he is falsely accused of murdering another con.

Sample Dialogue: "I've heard of some tough cans, but I guess this joint beats them all."

Hollywood Touch: Brady is saved from a death sentence by a hidden in-cell Dictaphone that captures the confession of the real killer.

Film Title: *King of Alcatraz,* directed by Robert Florey

Starring: Lloyd Nolan, Robert Preston, J. Carrol Naish

Year: 1938 (Paramount)

Plot: An escaped Alcatraz convict takes over a cruise ship.

Sample Dialogue: "Before I was sent to Alcatraz, I had four thousand men on my payroll. I had ten when I got out."

Hollywood Touch: Funny how

easy it is to break out of Alcatraz when the plot depends on it.

Film Title: *Prison Train*, directed by Gordon Wiles

Starring: Fred Keating, Linda Winters, Clarence Mules

Year: 1938 (Equity)

Plot: Gang leader and convicted murderer Frankie Terris finds that his Alcatraz-bound prison train carries a lot of people who want to see him dead.

Sample Dialogue: "Why Alcatraz? Why are they stickin' me on the Rock? What's the matter with Atlanta or Leavenworth? They're plenty tough!"

Hollywood Touch: The government's so eager to see Terris do his time that he gets his own personal G-man on board to make sure he reaches Alcatraz safely.

Film Title: *The House Across the Bay*, directed by Archie Mayo

Starring: George Raft, Joan Bennett, Lloyd Nolan, Walter Pidgeon

Year: 1940 (United Artists)

Plot: A showgirl tries to remain true to her gangster husband after he's sent to Alcatraz.

Sample Dialogue: "Get a load of those Rock widows over there. Together they got 500 years—with good behavior."

Hollywood Touch: No currents in *this* bay—gangster Steve Lowry practically breast-strokes to shore.

Film Title: *San Francisco Docks*, directed by Arthur Lubin

Starring: Burgess Meredith, Irene Hervey, Raymond Walburn

Year: 1941 (MCA/Universal Pictures)

Plot: A San Francisco longshoreman is arrested for a murder that was actually committed by an escaped Alcatraz prisoner.

Sample Dialogue: "What's the matter, you don't have those Alcatraz birds back there, do ya?"

Hollywood Touch: Escaping prisoners find a boat waiting for them just offshore—undeterred or undetected by the guards in the island watchtowers.

Film Title: *Seven Miles from Alcatraz,* directed by Edward Dmytryk

Starring: James Craig, Frank Jenks, Bonita Granville

Year: 1943 (RKO)

Plot: Two cowardly cons escape Alcatraz in fear of bombing attacks and end up defeating a Nazi spy ring at a nearby lighthouse.

Sample Dialogue: "They took their citizenship papers back the day they threw me on that Rock. . . . What did this country ever give me anyway, besides life?"

Hollywood Touch: These cons sleep two to a cell and swim from Alcatraz to a nonexistent lighthouse, and that's just in the first fifteen minutes.

Film Title: *Train to Alcatraz,* directed by Philip Ford

Starring: Don Barry, Janet Martin, William Phipps

Year: 1948 (Republic Pictures)

Plot: Convicts on a train to Alcatraz try to make a break.

Sample Dialogue: "We've got to make a break—they're taking us to Alcatraz! We'll be there for the rest of our lives! It's a fortress! A fortress, I tell you, sitting on a rock in the middle of the bay, with tides all around, waiting to grab you and pull you down!"

Hollywood Touch: The young convict hero is released from the prison train with a comely young passenger after getting a telegram from his lawyer saying someone else confessed to the crime that had sent him to the Rock.

Film Title: *Experiment Alcatraz,* directed by Edward L. Cahn

Starring: John Howard, Joan Dixon

Year: 1950 (RKO)

Plot: A scientist injects Alcatraz volunteers with a radioactive substance that might cure a rare blood disease. When one con kills another and blames it on the injection, the heroic scientist must prove the con had a more nefarious motive.

Sample Dialogue: "The Rock. A little iron curtain world of lost souls sitting in the shadow of the Golden Gate. Its inmates are felons the other prisons didn't want. That little stretch of water between Alcatraz and San Francisco is wider than the Pacific as far as the prisoners are concerned. They're not going to cross it unless they die or serve their time."

Hollywood Touch: Prisoners earn an unconditional release as soon as they receive the injection.

Film Title: *Alcatraz Express* or *The Big Train,* directed by John Peyser

Starring: Robert Stack, Neville Brand, Bruce Gordon

Year: 1962 (Paramount/Desilu)

Plot: Al Capone, terrified of being transferred to the Rock, tries to escape from the Alcatraz-bound prison train but is defeated by Elliot Ness and his heroic G-men.

Sample Dialogue: "Warden, this Alcatraz is for tough guys, not people like me. What did I ever do? Just show me on my record—I'm here on a lousy income tax deal. It's just not right! They can't do it!"

Hollywood Touch: In this movie, Elliot Ness is the brains behind the creation of Alcatraz Federal Penitentiary (United States Penitentiary, Alcaraz Island).

Film Title: *Birdman of Alcatraz,* directed by John Frankenheimer

Starring: Burt Lancaster, Karl Malden, Telly Savalas

Year: 1962 (United Artists)

Plot: Inmate Robert Stroud battles the soul-crushing conformity of prison life by raising birds.

Sample Dialogue:
REPORTER, as Stroud is released from Alcatraz: "Mr. Stroud, how does it feel to be out of Alcatraz?"
STROUD: "If you San Franciscans had any true civic pride, you'd blow the place out of the water instead of advertising it. What an eyesore."

Hollywood Touch: Lancaster's Stroud is a gentle soul and the author of a critique of the penal system. The real Stroud was violent and unpredictable and the author of a large collection of pornography.

Film Title: *Point Blank,* directed by John Boorman

Starring: Lee Marvin, Angie Dickinson, Carroll O'Connor

Year: 1967 (Metro-Goldwyn-Mayer)

Plot: After being double-crossed and left for dead in an Alcatraz cell by his unfaithful wife and her gangster boyfriend, a man seeks revenge and his stolen money.

Sample Dialogue: "That night on Alcatraz I knew it was you I really want. I found out too late."

Hollywood Touch: The hero swims from Alcatraz to shore, despite having just been shot.

Film Title: *Skidoo*, directed by Otto Preminger

Starring: Groucho Marx, Carol Channing, Jackie Gleason, Frankie Avalon

Year: 1968 (Paramount)

Plot: A retired gangster goes to Alcatraz to kill an inmate who plans to testify against the leader of a comical crime syndicate.

Sample Dialogue: "Senator, I can see it all! A perfect penitentiary. . . . My men are going to learn to express themselves! We're going to have finger painting and modern dance. . . . I'm going to teach them to make costume jewelry and they can even design their own uniforms!"

Hollywood Touch: The entire prison—the inmates, the warden, and all of the guards—end up high on LSD.

Film Title: *Alcatraz Breakout*, directed by Jan Anders

Starring: Gary Boyd, Sivi Walter, Aldo Girotti

Year: 1975 (Studio Unknown)

Plot: An Alcatraz inmate tries every possible way to escape.

Sample Dialogue: "With the Lord's help, I've built a penal institution here at Alcatraz Island that's a model which others follow. Unstable men—men like yourself, Grant, that can't adjust to society's rules—

have tried in the past to destroy it. But in the end, Alcatraz has always destroyed them. As it will you."

Hollywood Touch: The hero knocks out his own teeth one by one and uses them to file through the bars—who knew enamel could wear down steel?

Film Title: *The Enforcer*, directed by James Fargo

Starring: Clint Eastwood, Tyne Daly

Year: 1976 (Warner)

Plot: Terrorists kidnap the mayor of San Francisco and hide out on Alcatraz. Dirty Harry and a young female partner go to rescue them.

Sample Dialogue: "The mayor of this pig city has been taken as a prisoner of war by the People's Revolutionary Strike Force."

Hollywood Touch: The tower on the former army parade ground that Eastwood blows up at the end of the movie never existed in real life—it was constructed for the movie.

Film Title: *Escape from Alcatraz*, directed by Don Siegel

Starring: Clint Eastwood, Patrick McGoohan, Roberts Blossom

Year: 1979 (Paramount/Malpaso)

Plot: The story of the daring 1962 escape by Frank Morris and the Anglin brothers.

Sample Dialogue: "Alcatraz was built to keep all the rotten eggs in one basket. It's my job to see that the stink from the eggs does not escape. . . . No one has ever escaped from Alcatraz. And no one ever will."

Hollywood Touch: Most consider this the most accurate Alcatraz movie ever made. Still, only Clint Eastwood could dig through concrete with a spoon and weld metal using a pack of matches.

Film Title: *Alcatraz: The Whole Shocking Story,* directed by Paul Krasny (TV)
Starring: Michael Beck, Art Carney, Telly Savalas
Year: 1980
Plot: The story of Clarence Carnes, the youngest prisoner ever sent to Alcatraz.
Sample Dialogue: "Now, this is the Rock. You're here because you're useless and worthless, both in society and in the prison system. And here you'll stay until the day you die. Or you get paroled. There's no escape. Swim and the current will drown you or the sharks will eat you. Smart cons don't even try."
Hollywood Touch: The movie has Carnes helping the guards

who were held as hostages during the 1946 uprising and thus escaping the gas chamber after the riot is quelled. In reality, he got a lighter sentence than the other participants by testifying against them.

Film Title: *Kicks,* directed by William Wiard (TV)
Starring: Anthony Geary, Shelley Hack
Year: 1985
Plot: An adrenaline junkie hooks up with a handsome playboy for high-stakes games, but ends up being stalked by him as she tries to find an incriminating videotape hidden in an Alcatraz prison cell.
Sample Dialogue: "I'm going to go out to the island, I'm going to get the tape and that'll be the end of it."
Hollywood Touch: Somehow,

having people arrive on the island by speedboat in broad daylight and start shooting at each other doesn't attract the attention of the Alcatraz rangers.

Film Title: *Terror on Alcatraz,* directed by Philip Marcus

Starring: Aldo Ray, Veronica Porche Ali, Sandy Brooke

Year: 1987 (Trans-World)

Plot: Escaped inmate Frank Morris returns to present-day Alcatraz to find a map that will lead him to stolen money, and takes time out to slaughter a few tourists.

Sample Dialogue: "You think you're going to come back to an island of ghosts and kick ass?... This island kicked ass for thousands of years!"

Hollywood Touch: In the movie, Alcatraz hasn't been a functioning prison for more than twenty years, but Morris is still able to find a nice sharp meat cleaver in the prison kitchen.

Film Title: *Force of Darkness,* directed by Alan Hauge

Starring: Mel Novak, Douglas Alan Shanklin, Loren Cedar

Year: 1987 (GMT Studios)

Plot: A demon-possessed mental patient holes up in the abandoned Alcatraz prison.

Sample Dialogue: "And so the two-week standoff continues between park officials and the Board of Supervisors regarding the cancellation of public tours through Alcatraz.... Prior to the island's closing there were numerous complaints by frightened tourists who claimed to have experienced strange and unusual phenomena during recent visits."

Hollywood Touch: When they canceled the tours, the National Park Service apparently removed every stick of furniture from the cellhouse.

Film Title: *Slaughterhouse Rock,* directed by Dimitri Logothetis

Starring: Nicholas Celozzi, Tom Reilly, Donna Denton, Toni Basil

Year: 1987 (Arista)

Plot: A group of teens visits Alcatraz in the middle of the night to confront a malevolent spirit.

Sample Dialogue: "All tourist traffic across the Bay to Alcatraz Island was halted this morning by the US Forest Service in the wake of a bizarre episode which occurred on the island just before the last tourist group was supposed to return to shore around sunset. . . . The mangled remains of the group were discovered shortly before the group was scheduled to leave."

Hollywood Touch: The plot involves spooky Civil War-era Native American artifacts that are discovered lying in plain sight in the basement of the prison.

Film Title: *So I Married an Axe Murderer,* directed by Thomas Schlamme

Starring: Mike Myers, Amanda Plummer, Nancy Travis, Anthony LaPaglia

Year: 1993 (Fried/Woods/Tristar)

Plot: A bookstore owner thinks his fiancée might be an axe murderer.

Sample Dialogue: "Hello, everyone, I am a park ranger and I will be leading you on the tour. All of the park rangers here at Alcatraz were at one time guards, myself included. My name is John Johnson, but everyone here calls me Vickie. Will you please follow me?"

Hollywood Touch: While former guards have volunteered on the island, none have actually become NPS rangers.

Film Title: *Murder in the First,* directed by Marc Rocco

Starring: Christian Slater, Gary Oldman, Kevin Bacon

Year: 1995 (Warner Brothers)

Plot: A fictionalized account of the murder trial of Alcatraz inmate Henry Young.

Sample Dialogue: "Is it not true that these men were taken off the island in strait jackets and committed to mental institutions? Here are men who came to Alcatraz legally sane, were subjected to the conditions of Alcatraz, and then judged to be insane, is that not true?"

Hollywood Touch: In the movie, Henry Young is sent to Alcatraz after stealing $5 from a rural grocery store/post office to feed his starving sister. The real Henry Young was a bank robber and murderer.

And while the movie has him committing suicide in his cell, the real Henry Young jumped parole in 1972 and might even have lived to see the movie.

Film Title: *The Rock,* directed by Michael Bay

Starring: Sean Connery, Nicolas Cage, Ed Harris

Year: 1996 (Hollywood Pictures)

Plot: Terrorists hole up on Alcatraz and threaten to fire poison gas missiles at San Francisco.

Sample Dialogue: "Call the San Francisco office—it looks like Alcatraz just reopened."

Hollywood Touch: The underground tunnels Cage and Connery use to penetrate Alcatraz exist only in the imagination of a Hollywood screenwriter.

Film Title: *All Dogs Go To Heaven 2*, directed by Larry Leker, Paul Sabella

Starring: The voices of Charlie Sheen, Dom DeLuise, Sheena Easton, Ernest Borgnine

Year: 1996 (MGM-UA)

Plot: After an evil dog steals Gabriel's horn for the Devil, the dogs of heaven are imprisoned in the cells of Alcatraz.

Sample Dialogue: "Be a good little bow-wow and fetch me my horn."

Hollywood Touch: Alcatraz turns out to be Lucifer's own holding tank.

Film Title: *Half Past Dead*, directed by Don Michael Paul

Starring: Steven Seagal, Morris Chestnut, Ja Rule

Year: 2002 (Sony)

Plot: A gang breaks into the "New Alcatraz" prison to find the whereabouts of a death row inmate's cache of gold.

Sample Dialogue: "There's only one way off this rock, homeys. And that key is under my pillow."

Hollywood Touch: This Alcatraz has an on-site execution chamber. The real Alcatraz did not—men sentenced to death were executed at San Quentin.

The following were not reviewed:
Passport to Alcatraz (1940) Aside from the title, has nothing to do with Alcatraz.
Electric Dreams (1984) Has only one, very short, Alcatraz scene with no dialogue.

Not available for viewing:
Road to Alcatraz (1945)
Terror at Alcatraz (TV, 1987)
Six Against the Rock (TV, 1987)
Caged Heat 2: Stripped of Freedom (1994)

Fiction Collides with Fact

In its "Monday Morning Highlights" for 1/20/95, the Bureau of Prisons responded to the release of the movie Murder in the First *as follows. This is an abbreviated version; to read the full statement, visit www.bop.gov/ipapg/ipafirst. html. (Used with permission of the Bureau of Prisons)*

The Warner Brothers film *Murder in the First* claims to be "inspired" by the true story of Alcatraz inmate Henry Young. . . . Although Henry Young was indeed an inmate at Alcatraz who was convicted in 1941 of involuntary manslaughter in the stabbing death of fellow inmate Rufus McCain, the events depicted in the motion picture are almost wholly fictional. In particular, the premise of the movie—that Young was a nonviolent inmate who was tortured on Alcatraz and was thereby driven to kill someone—is completely false.

Murder in the First claims that Young was a teenage orphan who was sentenced to Alcatraz for stealing $5 from a grocery store in order to feed his starving sister, and that he "never harmed or attempted to harm anyone" before entering Alcatraz. The true story is that he was a bank robber who had taken and brutalized a hostage on at least one occasion and committed murder in 1933—some 3 years before being incarcerated at Alcatraz. He had served time in State prisons in Montana and Washington before entering Federal prison for the first time in 1935 at the U.S. Penitentiary on McNeil Island, Washington (which is now a State prison).

Although Young did participate in a January 1939 escape attempt, he was not kept naked in a dark dungeon for 3 years as punishment, as the movie indicates. Instead, he was held in the disciplinary segregation unit in the main cellhouse as punishment for the escape attempt. He was confined to a normal cell—not a dungeon—with plumbing, an electric light, a cot, and other appropriate cell furnishings. Various events in the movie set in a dungeon—such as scenes where the associate warden slashes Young's Achilles tendon to prevent future escapes—are fabrications. . . .

In reality, Young was released

from his cell in segregation after only a few months. He was returned to the general population no later than autumn 1939. More than a year after that—in December 1940—he killed McCain in the industries building.

The movie also implies that Young died on Alcatraz in 1942, evidently committing suicide after scrawling the word "victory" on the wall or floor of his cell. This is not true, either. Young remained at Alcatraz until 1948, when he was transferred to the Medical Center for Federal Prisoners at Springfield, Missouri. When his Federal sentence expired in 1954, he was turned over to the Washington State Penitentiary at Walla Walla to begin a life sentence for an earlier murder conviction. In 1972, he was released from Washington State Penitentiary, but he jumped parole and, according to Washington State authorities, his whereabouts are unknown. Far from committing suicide 53 years ago, therefore, Young might still be alive.

Many of the depictions of Alcatraz and its staff are completely inaccurate. *Murder in the First* portrays the warden as managing three prisons simultaneously: USP Alcatraz, and the California State prisons at Folsom and San Quentin. The movie further states that the warden visited Alcatraz only 24 times over a 3-year period. In fact, no one has been warden of a Federal prison and a State prison simultaneously. . . .

Nor is there any validity to claims that FBI Director J. Edgar Hoover selected Johnston to be warden at Alcatraz, that Hoover and the Alcatraz management intimidated prospective witnesses in Young's trial, that inmates were being driven insane at Alcatraz, and that 32 were removed from the island in straitjackets during a period of only a few years leading up to Young's trial. Equally groundless and unfair is the depiction of officers at Alcatraz as sadistic brutes. The evil prison officer is one of the oldest and least imaginative movie clichés, and one of the most misleading. The motion picture contained numerous other mistakes and misrepresentations.

STUDIO CREDITS

Frontis/title: Still, *The Rock* © Hollywood Pictures/Disney. Used with permission.

p. 5: Poster, *Road to Alcatraz* © Paramount Pictures. Used with permission.

p. 9: Still, *Birdman of Alcatraz* © 1962 Metro-Goldwyn-Mayer Studios Inc. All Rights Reserved. Courtesy of MGM CLIP+STILL. Used with permission. Burt Lancaster and related rights: © The Burt Lancaster 1988 Revocable Trust, used under license. Represented by The Roger Richman Agency, Inc. Used with permission.

p. 14: Poster, *Experiment Alcatraz* © RKO Pictures, licensed by Warner Bros. Entertainment Co. All Rights Reserved. Used with permission

p. 32 (bottom): Still, *The Last Gangster* © Turner Entertainment Co., a Warner Bros. Entertainment Company. All Rights Reserved. Used with permission. Edward G. Robinson and related rights: © The Edward G. Robinson Estate, used under license. Represented by The Roger Richman Agency. Used with permission.

p. 34: Poster, *Train to Alcatraz* © Paramount Pictures. Used with permission.

p. 36 (left): Still, *Murder in the First* © Warner Bros., a Division of Time Warner Entertainment Company, L.P., and Le Studio Canal+ (U.S.). All Rights Reserved. Used with permission.

p. 37 (bottom): Still, *Escape from Alcatraz* © Paramount Pictures/Malpaso. Used with permission.

p. 41: Poster, *House Across the Bay*. No known copyright holder at this time.

p. 45: Poster, *Seven Miles from Alcatraz* © RKO Pictures. Licensed by Warner Bros. Entertainment, Inc. All Rights Reserved. Used with permission.

p. 51: Poster, *Birdman of Alcatraz* © 1962 Metro-Goldwyn-Mayer Studios Inc. All Rights Reserved. Courtesy of MGM CLIP+STILL. Used with permission. Burt Lancaster and related rights: © The Burt Lancaster 1988 Revocable Trust, used under license. Represented by The Roger Richman Agency, Inc. Used with permission.

p. 54 (bottom): Still, *Escape from Alcatraz* © Paramount Pictures/Malpaso. Used with permission.

p. 57: Poster, *The Rock* © Hollywood Pictures/Disney. Courtesy Nicolas Cage, Sean Connery, Ed Harris. Used with permission.

p. 59: Still, *The Rock* © Hollywood Pictures/ Disney. Courtesy Sean Connery, Nicolas Cage. Used with permission.

p. 65 (bottom): Still, *Escape from Alcatraz* © Paramount Pictures/Malpaso. Used with permission.

p. 67: Poster, *Murder in the First* © Warner Bros. A Division of Time Warner Entertainment Company, L.P., and Le Studio Canal+ (U.S.). All Rights Reserved. Used with permission.

p. 72: Posters, *Escape from Alcatraz* © Paramount Pictures/Malpaso. Used with permission; *Skidoo* © Paramount Pictures. Courtesy Jackie Gleason Enterprises. Used with permission.